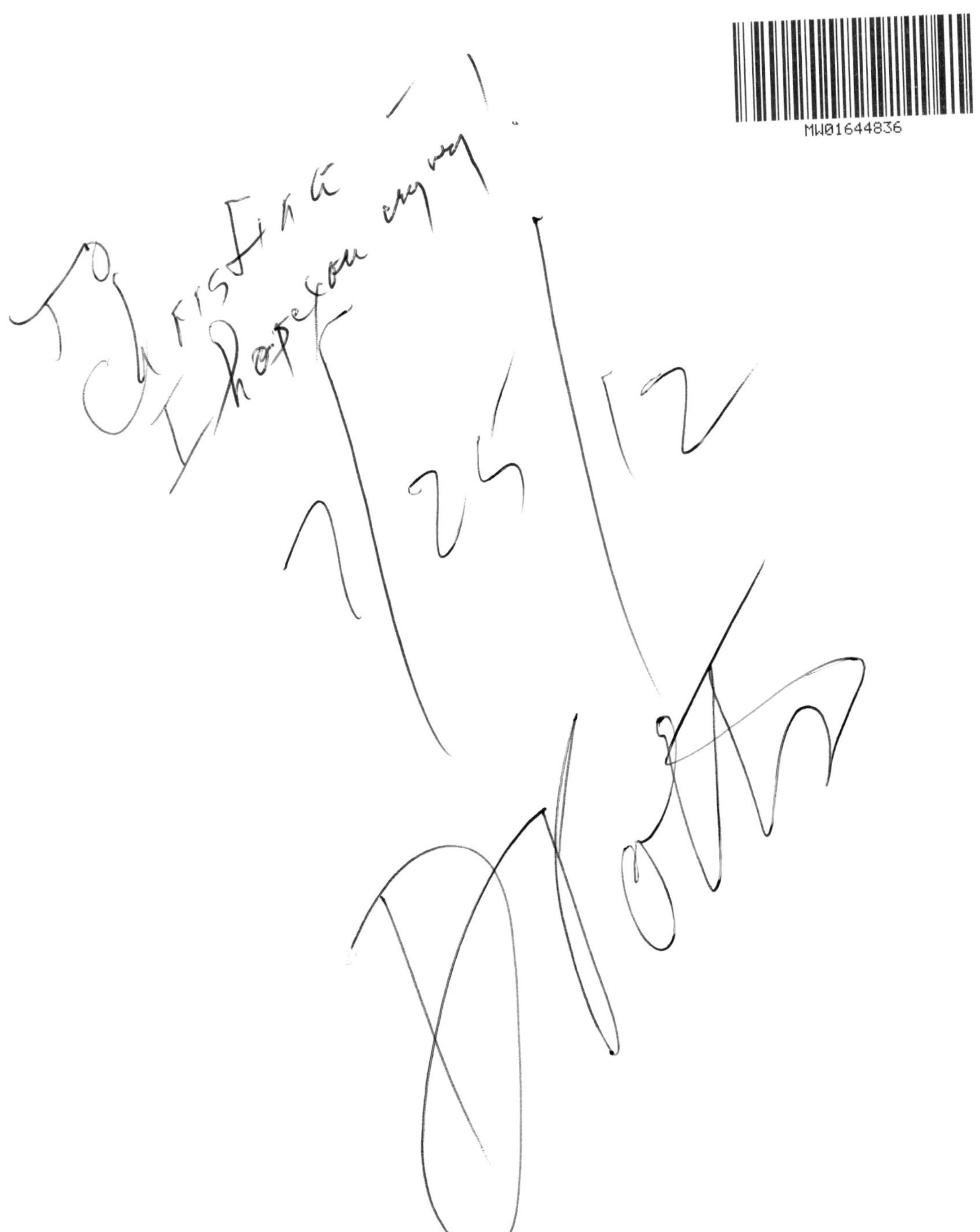

Soul Fire

Daniel C. Potts, M.D.

ISBN-13: 978-1469997179

CONTENTS

Poetry

DEDICATION

This book is dedicated in memory of my father, Lester Eugene Potts, Jr., an inspired artist of life's beautiful watercolors, who taught me that the cure for Alzheimer's disease is the human spirit itself. Likewise, it is dedicated to my mother, Ethelda Oaks Potts, Dad's tireless and loving primary caregiver. Furthermore, it is dedicated to all those persons living with Alzheimer's disease and dementia as well as their caregivers and to all who dignify humanity by their efforts to improve quality of life for those with cognitive disorders.

Photographs

ACKNOWLEDGEMENTS

Without the unconditional and up-building love and support of my wife, Ellen Woodward Potts, this book would not have been possible. She helped me to find my poetic voice. Additionally, the love of my two daughters, Julie and Maria Potts, makes my soul fire burn more warmly.

The photographs displayed here were made primarily on family trips. I thank my girls for granting me permission, though somewhat unwillingly at times, to risk life and limb for "the perfect shot."

FOREWORD

Soul fire, life's inextinguishable flame of the true self, burns throughout eternity with God-imparted energy. It warms the world with beauty and love; it sings and paints and dances and prays. Seeking energy in others and burning more brightly in relationship, it imparts but never gives out. It is fire of the divine spirit infused through flesh, and no frailty or affliction can douse it. Pure love is its infinite source.

It blazes with the colors of God. These same colors are seen in the wonders of our world: sunsets' glow, tender green of spring, ashen gray of clouds, vibrant hues of gardens, dark patterns in the grain of woods. "The Unseen Hand" paints from the reservoir of Heaven.

We must learn to feel this fire, to see these shades in others, to know them as eternal souls with cores of unfathomable elemental riches. Seeing their true selves, we must celebrate life in them, with them.

And if flesh or mind should fail, we must affirm the light within, seeking to spread its warmth and glow through deepened relationship. We must lift the torch of personhood for all.

This book is produced in celebration of the fire which burns in and through us and those we love, even in the grandeur of creation. It gives gratitude to God for personhood and kinship, and for the immeasurable gift of this world through which we may behold, even today, the creative mastermind at work.

My Heart

Come in.
The door isn't always open.

You listened. You cared. You knew my eyes.
That tripped the lock.

Be careful not to slip on dirty clothes.

I Am Here

I am here…
buried with the ballast
of discarded days.

Personhood
cowers in the carnage:
headlights through the haze.

Do you see?
Silver moon of swamp light
'luminates the land.

Look at me!
Rake away the refuse.
Hold me by the hand.

Probe the Heart

Don't dare say of me,
"There's nothing left to do."
Probe the heart you see
with loving eyes of you.

Muted Rays

Shining, speaking eyes…

lenses through which beams of mind and heart
converge on targets seeking to receive some message
from warmth of inner core
communicating life and love,
memories and hopes held-dear,
things vapor-light and dense as lead;
things cherished, dreaded, stoked within
as essence of the bluest blue
of flame that burns in heart and head;

whose muting hands enwrap your mouths
and draw a darkened shroud
of veil-like fingers down across
the self-soul's window pane?

Are these dark hands so dense, opaque
that dazzling inner sun beneath
can't sear its laser beam of light
and breach black holes now sinking in upon themselves
to trap all traces of the one
whom we still love, beneath?

No, in fact.
For though aphasic eyes
stare out through lightless glass,
their fading whispers scarce-perceived
by caring ears trained fast on them,

the radiance of this waning star
will warm the lives of those who love
light-years beyond the bygone day
its smoldering core has cooled.

Dumplin's

(a savory memory)

See me runnin'?
'Cross the field with my dress a-flyin'?
On my way to Grandmama's for some dumplin's.
Hers were the best, you know.
She said they were 'cause that's how much she loved me….

Their smell gits in my nose and makes my stomach roll over.
Settles in my head…I nearly trip from sprintin'.
But I go to skippin' with glee when I git close.
Guess my insides is skippin' too.

Outside her door now.
Lookin' through the winduh I can see her old flour-dusted apron.
(Dust my tummy with the flour when I'm there to help.)
She hears me clamor for the door and hollers
"Come git 'em honey, I'm just takin' 'em up!"

Little slivery, shiny tasty things
swimmin' with chicken in a bubbly broth.
Shake me out some pepper and dip in my spoon…
Mmm Mmm!!
I love you Grandmama! And I love your savory, shiny little dumplin's…
They make me feel good right this minute…

"Look, she's responding a little."

"What are you thinking about sweetie?"

("I thought she was out of it")

"That's the first time I've seen her smile in weeks."

"Wonder if she knows us…who is this Grandmama?"

"Bless her heart."

"OK, what's taking so long? Pass them down here!"

"Hey Mom, they sure are shiny."

"You must have followed Grandmama's recipe."

Skippin' Rocks

It seems to me
that in these budgetary days of making every moment count
toward something we perceive of worth in some material sense,
not near enough is made of standing on some creek or riverbank
(or by a pond, perhaps),
and skippin' rocks.

Oh, I know just what a part of you would say;
the part of me that's dressed in widget-counting garb
and skims from task to task barely breaking life's surface,
and tries to keep ahead of "who's its' at the club"
would say the same:
what gain, what accolade could come
from standing idly on some bank
and skippin' rocks?

In answer, let's remind ourselves of where we came to be:
upon a rocky interface, as waters first kissed hardened shore,
and there the primal life of earth brushed over skippin' stones
smoothed-slick by ceaseless flow of tides.

No wonder, then, we're drawn to rock-strewn shores of waters' edge,
much as we've always been,
to feel again the touch of terra firma,
awakening genetic memories long buried in sediment and sand.

What's that you say?
Oh no, no sacrilege my statements constitute.
For I am both creationist and evolutionist
and dare not relegate God to boxes made with human hands.

From our shallow contemporary existence
we need escape to waters' edge
to hear again that tripping shoreline melody,
to have again our souls caressed by swirling eddies,
to feel again those polished stones…

Papa showed me how to choose:
of course, the smoothest ones were valued most,
as these would glide so nearly free of friction's grasp
and sail the closest toward the lofty goal of farther shore.
Some weight was needed, else the slivered wisp
would catch a gust and fly downstream without a single skip.
It's hard to underestimate the value of trajectory:
with angle too acute one skip's the most you'd get.
With one too wide your stone would take a first-glance dive.
From Papa's hand, it always seemed
the perfect rock was borne aloft in perfect path
to send it skipping endlessly
across the skim to distant shoreline
(a goal to which I yet aspire
and fail more 'oft than not, I must admit).
And with each flawless fling
our praise and affirmation freely flowed
toward his section of the bluff.

Of late, as more and more of Papa's life bank
crumbles, clod-like, into swiftly flowing currents,
times of skippin' rocks are left as isles of happiness on which to rest.
In latter days not much brings sparkle to his gaze.
But searching, hurling, skippin' never fails to find its goal:
to briefly touch the Farther Shore,
and there, the soul.

And little ones, seeking paternal praise,
search diligently for smoothest stones,
soliciting help at times,
and awkwardly heave pebble hints in Papa's wake.

So, what gain, what accolade could come
from standing idly on some bank
and skippin' rocks?

None, I guess, unless...
Some value is ascribed to
reaching back across the sands of time
to feel a texture first felt then;
to descending from mountains of materialism
toward a spot where worth is sensed with hands and hearts alone;
to viewing our lives once more through idealistic childhood eyes;
to standing near the ones we love
to laugh with them,
and praise,
and bless.

The White-washed Fence

He built it not to keep things out
(except, perhaps, the honeysuckle vines
which incessantly launched their fragrant conquests
out into his pristine lawn)
nor hem things in,
(though a man of boundaries
I've known him to be).

By Great Depressions' yardstick he was reared to use
to size-up value in a thing
it couldn't really measure up,
for standing post-like on the fringe
it didn't give a hard-days' work
or save a nickel for its kin.

You see, within the wooden fiber of his frame
he felt one must be tirelessly about one's tasks,
producing self-sufficient wares without an ounce of waste.
Labor purely for aesthetic wage
was vainly spent, it seemed to him.

Why, then, did he search out fence posts, nails and boards
and toil so diligently in Alabama summer sweat
to make an idle fence?

I feel he did in part because he longed to build.
So crafty with his tools was he

that few repairmen ever set one foot within his realm.
He never could stay far away from wood, as well,
for shelter, food and childhood's clothes
were bought outright without a debt
by lumber planed and woodchips shorn
just back behind the smokehouse
in the old sawmill.

And, then, there was the pride he took in keeping up the yard.
Folks around still speak about the beauty of it.

However, in my heart I know
these weren't the purest motives for his work,
for hammer never would have struck
nor white-washed paintbrush stroked
if not for sacrificial love
implanted like a post within his red-clay soil.

He sought to make surroundings fine and fair for his dear wife,
as deep within he knew he'd found
a rare and fragrant flower of graceful vine
caught winding 'round his planks of wood in younger days.

And for his boy, of course,
he yearned to pass along his craftsmanship,
to teach the young one how to build
and how to give a helpful hand
to those with whom he'd be called to task,
and so provide a summer thrill
to a restless, cherished gift that tagged along.

He was himself, in no small way
like something planted in a red clay hill,
secured to stand upright and firm
by packing down around his base,
as boots and up-turned shovel ends
of loving kin had labored long,
foundations to provide for him and progeny to come.

The fence he built, much like the man, was kept in good repair:
no sagging planks allowed, no leaning posts,
no mildewed shades of white.
Its boards held back life's tangled weeds
and marked the hallowed ground of home
to set example fine for those who chanced to look his way.

As will come to most of us
his time for leaving home place came some years ago.
I took opportunity the other day
to pass it by, that holy site of childhood relics
lain to rest in packy catacombs of clay.
The fence (of sorts) still stood there on the fringe,
though not as I remember it;
for now its tilting, brownish posts
push out the nails which held his well-planed planks so close,
and fractured on the row lie rotting boards
among the greedy, viny legions no more thwarted
by the boundaries that he laid.

I left that place and came to visit him in dwelling new.
Repairs were needed on the garden gate,
and so we gathered up his well worn tools
and headed to the chore.
But now it is the boy who lays his hammer to the nail;
it has to be, you see,
for decay of dreaded scourge has breached his treated timbers.
Dexterity departed, he requires patient coaching
just to simply hold my plank,
and wanders off into the yard before the job's complete.

And so it now becomes my honored task to shore up fences.
I'll try to use the craftsmanship bequeathed to me
so lovingly through faithful hands
to straighten rails, refasten planks,
and splash fresh coats of whitewash all along the rows.
Instruction's echoes serve me well
as I lay heel and shovel's end
to firm up soil around each post.
For though I've traveled far from childhood's hallowed grounds
some cloddy clay stuck to my soul,
implanting new lawns with sanctifying memories
of earlier fence-building days.

Through Little Girls' Eyes

Beneficent Creator God,
show me your world through little girls' eyes
and with dainty fingers wind my heart
to play doxology in virgin wonderment.

Each glance
on glistening green prelude of spring
make as my first,
and every sharp-edged stone
an ancient arrowhead upon my path.

Train my ears
upon a chatty mockingbird's disguise
to hear its true and hidden voice beneath.

Implant afresh in me
desire to scale the greatest boulders
you have scattered on a bank,
and give trusted guardrail hands
to help me in my climb.

Keep my vision keen
to spot the little mud-brown toad
in startled hop toward leafy shelters off the path,
and stay my hands to cup him lightly
so to sense the slightest twitch,

but not to crush or smother
even though so soft a grip
might not thwart his freedom's leap.

And quicken then my feet
to run and tell the treasures
little eyes have found
on every Sabbath pilgrimage
into the wonderland of spring.

Lullai, Little One

"This day to you"

(who sing on hills, who seek in vales, who thirst by streams)

"is born a Child"

(to hear the song, to end the search, to hold the cup)

"of Mary, meek,"

(the favored one, a punctured heart, Magnificat)

"the virgin mild."

(a mother's love for winter warmth; the spring of life.)

"That blessed bairn"

(the Father's gift to every child: an only Son)

"so loving, kind,"

(the Father's heart in every cry: salvation's voice)

"shall now rejoice"

(a star for kings, a crook for lambs, Mysterium)

"both heart and mind."

(the mother's heart, the Father's mind, the Spirit's flesh…)

"Baloo Lammy."

A Light

A light, the manger lit.
Shepherds' night eyes, known only to the hills,
glowed warmly to beasts
and to the Heavenly Host.

Furrowed faces, 'trenched in toil,
met rows of angels toe to toe.
Each saber was a song,
And "Gloria"echoed in the heart.

Their eyes, as distant moons, drew near to orb' the Star;
the Son, hidden in the bushel of a barn.

Emmanuel, the Brother Lamb,
cried out among them.
His face, like theirs, with life lines-laid
beneath an infant's skin.

In that star's light
all eyes glowed like His.
And Light of light
revealed a Mother's love.

Though night was cold,
within this flock was warmth enough
for all.

Through Shining Eyes

O magnum mysterium, et admirabile sacramentum,
ut animalia viderent Dominum natum,
jacentem in praesepio!

(O great mystery, and wonderful sacrament,
that animals should see the new-born Lord, lying in a manger!)
Ironic. Unfathomable. Mysterious.

The world waits in woeful pangs, writhing for the Gift.
The seekers, learned watchers of the stars,
sense incubating warmth, and turn to face its glow.

Shepherds, tuned to trumpets in the hills,
steer flocks toward the bleating of a Lamb.

The Virgin and her King don cloaks of hay,
no room to be found.

Earth splits wide in silence
for this meteoric settling,
this clash of earth and Heaven
beneath a baby's fingertips.

And through shining eyes of brother-beasts
the Sacrament is given,
the Gift received,
jacentem in praesepio.

To Soar

Today,
emblazoned by the sun
and borne aloft by love,
you fly.

We sense
the gushing forth of you
into your wings.

For this moment
you were born, and so were we.
To soar.

Eternal Hues

A thousand million hues conceived within each sunset's womb
are birthed upon our autumn sky, and nestle in its coombe.
And each successive tint near-imperceptibly is merged
with kindred briefly set upon horizon's cusp, then purged.

If possible to tease apart the essence of each shade,
to isolate component-prime of each before it fades,
I feel the colors found would ne'er before have been revealed,
behind the veil 'twixt Heaven and earth forevermore concealed.

But, thankfully, for us who take the time at long days' end
to search the skies where earthly scenes and those of Heaven blend,
a gracious glimpse is given of a sight oft' unperceived:
eternal hues' brief earthly lives...our treasure to receive.

Mysteries

Comfort from embers in the cold.
Stillness in songs of flowing water.
Communion through confessions of the heart.
Safety in a little child's embrace.

Light from candles in our darkest room.
Home in eyes that know us.
Life through laying down our own.
Heaven in a sunset's pondering.

Understanding from stories shared.
Learning in the search to find ourselves.
Unity through caring for the hurt.

Love from being broken down.

Hold Me

(for Anna Gordon and the victims of the tornados of 4-27-2011)

Hold me…
lift me in your spirit arms and hold me.

It was bad…
so very bad; and dark, and terrible.
A night of silent screaming.
Did you hear? Did you know?
Could you feel me reaching?
Did you see it in my eyes
when you were close,
so close I felt your breath?

And then you came to me; came running, flying…
Your arms, your wings outstretched.
You called my name with your eyes.
Whispered weeping; a trumpet blast.

Bursting forth, alive to you again,
I scattered the rubble of entombment
as the vortex of your might uplifted me.

Now I spin toward home,
shedding death's debris in flight.
And when I land in your embrace
I will be me for the very first time.

Pentecost

Are You there?
Do You know what this is, this Hellish fury?
This swirling Satan in a cloud?
Was it You?
Did You unleash a Titan on Your children?
Perhaps You let us do it to ourselves. We are guilty.
I wonder...

But then I see it: the Face; the kind eyes.
Pure, sweet compassion in a gaze, shining out
to warm me; to save me;
to tear away the rubble bars and free me;
to wipe away the blood and tears;
both from my face
and Yours.

And first light tells the truth:
the roof collapsed....on You.
Glass shards, splintered wood and fiberglass
ripped You.
"Baby Doe 1, and 2, and 3, and unknown"
were You.
Fractured first-responder hearts;
childless parents' cries
were Yours.

And overalls, and baby shoes,
and T-shirts, and girdles,
and Sunday hats, and blue jeans,
and bathrobes, and sport coats
adorned You.

And bottled water quenched Your thirst,
and peanut butter fed You.
And chainsaws sang a song of praise.

And the Still Small Voice
echoed something like a freight train.

Exsanguination

Heart…

Please don't bleed anymore.

You studied medicine
and know a pump needs something to pump.
Without that something,
you are nothing.

With no bloody flood,
no influx of living flow,
your contractions are in vain.

Think of all the cells that need you,
that live because of your "lub-dub!"

Don't bleed out.
Don't desert them.

Don't desert me.

The Peace

Sweating through the slog
I trudge on.

Night lengthens:
rest is rarely won.

Then,
drawn by light and hue,
I "look to the hills"...

Help comes
from the Maker
who paints peace again.

The Two Guests

Within…
'midst smells of well-worn books and wine
and creamy candle smoke and scents of dinnertime

this room…
bids wary welcome to a guest
whose entry stills each motion of the heart and breast.

the air…
though stifled in a steely calm,
(oppression's voice anointing with a healing balm)

is warmed
beneath the Hand that offers Life,
and, by its very Elements, dispels the strife.

The Dance

(For Mother and the caregivers)

You beckoned me back then
to join you in dancing
upon a floor made clear for us
to have our moment in the waltz.

Perhaps you heard it first, then I:
the sameness of the string tunes played
by strumming hands upon our hearts,
drawing us with every finger stroke
in seamless unison toward the floor of dreams.

String-songs merged melodiously
as our hands first clasped
and gazes locked into the warm ensemble
which became the rhythm of our newfound joy.

So certain was your step, so deft your lead
across all reaches of the floor
I felt uneasiness depart, and with closing eyes
let myself be swept aloft by arms
which bade me out a moment past
from new life's fringe.

As symphonies of dreams seem to play unendingly
though but a solitary phrase has passed,
so the moment of our waltz went on and on.

Through pianos and fortes, allegros and andantes
we glided gracefully with steps both light and firm.
Other would-be waltzers
gazed at us with wishful eyes,
hoping their appointed time to take the floor
would be as ours had been.

And then, as a ritard began
which ushers in the swan song of each pair
I sensed the slightest changes in your step…
No longer purposeful and sure
you seemed to hesitate for me;
to need the warmth of other feet as guide,
those familiar with your stride
who'd danced the steps you'd made with them
in life's waning waltz.
At first you tried to hold the lead,
to take the steps innately yours.
But, wavering, you gazed at me with speaking eyes
while you still knew,
while you still could,
and through the music of our song
asked me to lead us to our rest at dancing's end.

And so I did.

The steps I made did not appear to me as deft
and graceful as the ones that led me

out from youth's uncertainties
onto life's polished hardwood floor.
But turning back upon our dancing time
as one rewinds a music box
to watch the gliding figures thereupon
in twirling, ebbing embrace,
an unexpected revelation comes:

The purest beauty of our dance
is that we listened for life's song for us,
and hearing harmonies within,
yielded to their sound.

And then, when half of our completed whole
no longer had the mind to yield
life's truest grace broke forth upon the floor:
the soul's own song of selfless love
triumphantly revealed
in feeble, faltering steps of dance.

I Weep

(John II: I-44)

I see him...
my brother,
dancing on the Holy Hills.

He prays,
he sings the soul song,
a ballad with the meter of His heart.

He is whole,
and the wholeness of him
prays and sings
and dances on the Hills,
with mansions and palaces in view.

And I feel the Peace;
surpassing, enwrapping all that is, eternally.

I feel it with him, in unity complete;
My Father at the joining point of souls,
the place where we are knit,
tethered in;
drawn together in the Truth, in the Life
that is All in All forever.

This is what I left.
This is why I came:
my brothers', sisters' union
with the Father's heart.
The linking of all
in Love Divine.

So why must it be?
why must he be wrapped again
in rags that wreak of death?

Not My will, but Thine.

I weep...
for glory given up.

Lazarus, come forth!

Broken Halleluiah

(Inspired by Leonard Cohen's "Halleluiah")

I've heard you had a secret art,
an exhibition of the heart
that pleased the Lord
as He could see right through ya'.
But did you know before the spell,
the cruel curse (a living Hell)
that in your soul you'd painted "Halleluiah?"
Halleluiah, Halleluiah...
Halleluiah, Halleluiah.

We saw the righteous way you stood
and showed your marbled grain of wood
to all who took a hallowed place next to ya'.
But even we who knew you well
could not imagine or foretell
that in your heart was painted "Halleluiah."
Halleluiah, Halleluiah...
Halleluiah, Halleluiah.

The devastation of your mind
and shattered mem'ries left behind
compelled the ones who cared to come rescue ya'.
Then strangely, through an opened door
an artist saw your spirit soar
and helped the hand to paint its "Halleluiah."
Halleluiah, Halleluiah...

Halleluiah, Halleluiah.

Such beauty we had never known,
created by your hands alone,
had power to bring dignity back to ya'.
And though we sometimes saw you smile
we knew the hurt within the trial
had made your art a broken "Halleluiah."
Halleluiah, Halleluiah…
Halleluiah, Halleluiah.

And now that you have flown away
to where we'll meet again someday
and stand in awe of One who always knew ya',
in words and art you've left behind
those shattered pieces of the mind,
composing us a healing "Halleluiah".
Halleluiah, Halleluiah…
Halleluiah, Halleluiah.

"I did my best (it wasn't much),
I couldn't think, so I tried to touch.
I told the truth; I didn't come to fool ya'.
And even though it all went wrong,
I stand before the Lord of Song
with nothing on my tongue but 'Halleluiah!'
Halleluiah, Halleluiah…
Halleluiah, Halleluiah."

Soul Fire

Just as the twig of oak,
though singed to soot by winter-burn
gropes upwardly with the pulsing sap of life,

so, too, the blighted mind,
though darkened like a wintry wick
burns outwardly with the inner fire of souls.

Remember

Remember who you are, my child,
who you were born to be;
let love be law in mind and heart,
let life be charity.

If bandaged, begging hands assail
your palisades of calm,
let labor bring tranquility,
let healing be its balm.

When death, itself, so stealthily
advances through your days,
let quiet faith be your resolve,
let living be your praise.

Then when my spirit and my flesh
unknit, and I am gone,
within your heart the finest part
of me continues on.

Seasoned Grain

Experience,
like sandpaper
rounds off freshly-cut ridges
to show
life's seasoned grain.

ABOUT THE AUTHOR

Daniel C. Potts, M.D. is a noted neurologist, author, educator and champion of those with Alzheimer's disease and other dementias and their caregivers. He was chosen by the American Academy of Neurology as the 2008 Donald M. Palatucci Advocate of the Year. Inspired by his father's transformation from saw miller to watercolor artist in the throes of dementia through person-centered care and the expressive arts, Dr. Potts seeks to make these therapies more widely available through his foundation, Cognitive Dynamics (www.cognitivedynamics.org). Additionally he is passionate about promoting self-preservation and dignity for all persons with cognitive impairment.

Made in the USA
Charleston, SC
20 July 2012